JULIE AND DEBBIE'S GUIDE TO GETTING RICH ON JUST $10 A WEEK !

JULIE AND DEBBIE'S GUIDE TO GETTING RICH ON JUST $10 A WEEK !

How We're Making a Fortune—and You Can Too—Using Dividend Re-Investment Plans

Deborah Rosen Barker
Julie Behr Zimmerman
Illustrator: Sheila S. Behr

D T P
Trade Paperbacks

A DELL TRADE PAPERBACK

Published by
Dell Publishing
a division of
Bantam Doubleday Dell Publishing Group, Inc.
1540 Broadway
New York, New York 10036

Book design by Susan Maksuta-Santoro

Library of Congress Cataloging in Publication Data
Barker, Deborah Rosen.
Julie and Debbie's guide to getting rich on just $10 a week! : how we're making a fortune—and you can too—using dividend reinvestment plans / Deborah Rosen Barker, Julie Behr Zimmerman ; illustrator, Sheila S. Behr.
p.   cm.
ISBN 0-440-50781-2
1. Investments—Handbooks, manuals, etc.   I. Zimmerman, Julie Behr.
II. Title.
HG4527.B238   1996
332.6—dc20   96-9689
                                                 CIP

Printed in the United States of America

Published simultaneously in Canada

March 1997

10   9   8   7   6   5   4

BVG

Dedication

To my children, Abby, Jason, and Nicole, for whose
support and love I will always be grateful.
To Steven, my husband and best friend.
J.B.Z.

In loving memory of Audrey Bowes Barker. With love
and gratitude to my children, Lilly, Jordan, Julie, and
Chris, and my husband, John. To Sandra and Richard
Rosen for their unfailing love and support, and to my
parents, Darrell and Inez Fritts, for giving me the
courage to feel that I could accomplish anything in life.
D.R.B.

Contents

CONTENTS

Money makes money, and the money
that money makes, makes more
money.

Ben Franklin

JULIE AND DEBBIE'S GUIDE TO GETTING RICH ON JUST $10 A WEEK !

OR, WHY TWO STAY-AT-HOME MOMS DON'T STAY AT HOME ANYMORE!

Before we had husbands, children, car pools, homework, piano lessons, PTA, and endless scout meetings, we had professional lives. However, we chose to leave the field of investment banking to be stay-at-home moms.

Five years and thirty pounds later our husbands were still at work, our children were now at school, and we were still at home—waiting for our families to come home to give our lives meaning.

One day we met at the health club for our dreaded workout; both of us figured if we had the body of Christie Brinkley and the perky attitude of Katie Couric, we would finally be happy.

And that's when the revelation hit us. Since the transformations we so craved were not occurring, we realized we had to develop some new goals to achieve happiness.

We got right off that treadmill and went to do what we thought we did best—*eat!*

Over breakfast our conversation drifted from children to husbands to food to current events, back to children, and finally rested on the stock market. We had left the industry for numerous reasons. While there, however, we felt our largest contribution had been helping others learn about investments. We both loved the simple joy of teaching displaced homemakers how to budget, and retired grandmothers that investing can be fun.

It then occurred to us that the general public, if they knew, could begin a savings plan by purchasing stock in a public company for as little as $10 a week without a stockbroker. Well, for the first time on record we didn't order more hash browns; we were too caught up in discussing our new idea. Just think of all the waitresses, secretaries, file clerks, junior executives, moms, dads, doctors, lawyers, and household engineers—in other words anyone and everyone—who never dreamed that

they could own stock for as little as $10 a week. And most of them had no idea that the opportunity was available to them.

How about the many grandparents who spend money (nickels and dimes) for candy and fast food to gratify their grandchildren? Not to mention the gifts these same grandparents give their grandchildren for birthdays or holidays. Now they could give a gift that literally keeps on giving—stock. Why not take the same money and buy stock in those companies instead?

One of our favorite stories we share at our seminars is about the grandparent who gave her grandchild stock in the Wrigley Corporation for his birthday. Not only did the grandchild receive stock in the company and dividends from the company's profits, but at Christmas he received a carton in the mail with twenty packs of gum from Wrigley. For the past nine years he thought about Grandma at Christmas when his carton of gum arrived. Talk about a stock that just keeps on giving and giving. (It reminds us of the Energizer Bunny that keeps going and going and going.)

During one of our seminars a nine-year-old boy announced that his grandmother had given him a birthday present that happened to be one share of stock in his local community power company. Yes, we were a bit taken aback, as we do not expect many children in this age group to own stock. However, we continued to listen to the wonderful child explain his interest in his stock. He proceeded to tell us how he was getting in trouble with his parents because he always left the lights on in his room (translated, his parents preached to him that this caused their electricity bill to go up substantially). Since he became a stockholder in the electric company, he decided to teach his parents a lesson in economics! He now reasoned that by leaving his lights on in his room, they would receive a higher electric bill, which would mean that the utility company would be making more money. If the company made more money, then he would receive a bigger dividend check.

Try arguing this logic with a very bright nine-year-old stockholder—better still, don't waste your breath—*he will win.* Why? Because you have always told him how much money it costs to leave his lights on in his room (even though we all know it represents a minimal cost), but logically how are you going to argue his point now that he owns part of the electric company? Sometimes parents just can't win—accept it and go on!

Twenty years from now those children and grandchildren are far more likely to enjoy and benefit from the gift of stock than to reminisce over a plastic toy, a special candy bar, or a pair of Rollerblades.

Suddenly we knew what we wanted to do. We put down our forks, picked up pencil and pad, and began to figure out a way that we could pass this information on to others. We had found a new challenge. Suddenly eating, exercising, carpooling, and cooking dinner became secondary.

We developed a user-friendly workbook and began conducting seminars designed to take the mysteries out of buying stock, even for those on a shoestring budget.

The response to the seminars has been overwhelming. We came to the conclusion that we needed a way to reach *more* people—that's why we wrote this book.

Reading this book is intended to be your first step. By the time you've finished, you'll be on your way to making the most of your hard-earned dollars through investing in the stock market for as little as $10 a week.

So let's get started!

INTRODUCTION

OR,
WHAT ABOUT ANNE?

In the course of conducting seminars on the how-tos of purchasing stocks without a broker, we have discovered a number of things about our audiences.

First of all our audiences are a diverse group of people—some as young as seven, some older than dinosaurs, some yuppie types, the Generation X-ers, secretaries, file clerks, blue-collar, no-collar, investment geniuses, know-it-alls, know-nothings, a smattering of Marilyn Monroes and Paul Newmans, and a lot of Attila the Huns.

Some people are truly interested in our seminar and want to learn as much as they can, while others sit through the introduction as if they are being given a course in quantum physics.

However, all this changes when we get to the story about Anne Scheiber. Suddenly our audience is transformed: Everyone listens, the doodling stops, and time stands still. Anne's story never fails to capture *everyone's* imagination. So if you had any doubts about reading a book on the stock market and were unsure whether you could suffer through such a dry, technical, and boring subject, lay your fears to rest and let us tell you about Anne. . . .

Anne Scheiber was an employee of the Internal Revenue Service in New York City for twenty-three years. She primarily audited the returns of the very wealthy. Anne was a very dedicated employee, yet she never received the accolades she so deserved, nor did she ever earn more than $4,000 a year. She attributed her lack of promotion at the IRS to her ethnicity and to the fact that she was a female.

So in 1944, at the age of fifty, she left the IRS, took her lifetime savings of $5,000, and retired to live the balance of her life in a rent-stabilized studio apartment on West Fifty-sixth Street in New York City. One thing Anne brought from her job with the IRS was the realization that a lot of money was made in the 1930s and 1940s through investments in the stock market.

Anne had a fascination with the movie studios at the time, and she took her $5,000 and invested it in entertainment stocks. She became consumed with studying the stock market. She never dated; she rarely left her apartment except to visit her stockbroker. She lived very frugally until her death in January 1995, at the age of 101.

Her investment strategies were simple. She did not worry about the day-to-day fluctuations in the stock market, nor did she have an interest in making a quick buck. Her philosophy was to choose high-quality companies that she knew, stay with those companies on a long-term basis, and most importantly *reinvest the dividends.* This interest in the stock market kept her entertained for the next fifty-one years.

Okay—so what about Anne?

Remember her original $5,000 investment? Even though she never added any money out of her pocket, it grew!

In fact, the economists at Yeshiva University could not believe how much it grew. You see, at her death that original investment of $5,000 had grown to *$22 million,* which she generously donated to Yeshiva University!

Fascinating story, but you're probably thinking one of two things at this point. First of all, what if you don't have $5,000 for that initial investment? And your second thought is that Anne used a stockbroker.

You're right on both counts. But we'll show you how to overcome these obstacles so that you, too, can spend a long, productive life being entertained (and enriched!) by the stock market.

Notes

HOW DO I SURVIVE WITHOUT A STOCKBROKER WHEN I DON'T KNOW THE FIRST THING ABOUT INVESTING?

Should I Buy a Crystal Ball?

Many people think that the only way to invest in the stock market is by using the services of a stockbroker and/or financial planner. Others believe that they need to accumulate thousands of dollars before they can even think about investing. Still others are just too intimidated by the "mysteries" of the stock market. Let's examine the validity of these excuses.

First of all, who are stockbrokers and financial planners? A *stockbroker* is an individual who is licensed and registered by the Securities and Exchange Commission. Stockbrokers can be employed by major stock brokerage firms, such as Merrill Lynch, A. G. Edwards, Charles Schwab, Fidelity, Quick & Reilly, and others.

A *financial planner* is someone who specializes in all aspects of an individual's finances, from insurance needs to retirement plans. Each time you buy or sell stock, you pay a commission. A portion of that commission goes to your broker or financial planner. The rest goes to the firm to cover costs.

Stockbrokers and financial planners earn their living by selling products. Each time they sell a product—stocks, bonds, elephants, or whatever—they receive a fee. In other words they receive a fee or commission for stocks that they sell and you purchase.

Think about this fact. If you are not buying or selling, they are not making money.

Now look at the second misconception: the idea that you need thousands of dollars in order to invest in the market. This is reverse-order thinking. You want to invest so that you can *make* thousands of dollars. What better vehicle than a plan where you can add a few dollars a week?

Many stock companies will let you invest as little as $10 a week without a broker. Granted, a $10-a-week investment will not grow into thousands of dollars by next month. But let's look at it another way: Had you not invested the $10 a week, would you be able to account for that money next month? Probably not. Probably it went toward movies, junk food, cosmetics, or whatever it is you saw in the store window when you were out during your lunch hour.

Is there an alternative? Yes! Start saving now and plan for the future. After all, as we grow older, we may still want to see those movies, buy cosmetics, and play golf, but not at the expense of having to starve!

Now it's time to address the mysteries of the stock market. Relax, put your feet up, and have your favorite snack. This is a no-brainer!

There are no "mysteries" in learning how to invest in the stock market. It can be compared to many other things we have learned in our lives.

Let's compare purchasing stock from a stockbroker

with purchasing an automobile from a car salesman. Is your first step to research the credentials, education, and experience of the salesman? Probably not.

Would you go to the car lot, tell him how much money

you can spend, give him the money, and allow him to choose the automobile for you?

Of course not. You'd take an active part in purchasing your automobile.

Or if you were to relocate to another town, would you open the Yellow Pages of the phone book, pick out a real estate agency with the prettiest ad, call them up, give them your money, and ask them to purchase the best house in the town for you?

Doubtful. Most of us would never dream of allowing a complete stranger to exercise this much control over our purchases. But this is what we expect stockbrokers and financial planners to do! The first step is to learn that just as we make decisions on where to live, how to dress, what to eat, and how to spend our money, we *can* make decisions about our financial futures too. And there's no need for a crystal ball.

Now comes the crystal-ball theory. Take a deep breath

and sit down, since this may be somewhat shocking: STOCKBROKERS *DO NOT* OWN CRYSTAL BALLS!

So you don't have a crystal ball either. That makes you no different from a stockbroker. But there is one thing they do have that you don't: knowledge about specific stocks. Without this knowledge you may find it difficult to make a purchase decision or even to know where to start.

Again, it is time to relax and reflect on the skills and

knowledge you already possess. Making your own in-vestment decisions is far less frightening than handing money over to a complete stranger (a stockbroker) and giving him permission to invest it for you.

Here are some things to consider in how to choose a stock.

Let's take a trip to the grocery store. If four of the five cereals *you* purchase are made by Kellogg's, which cereal company would you want to own stock in?

You're still in the grocery store, but now you're stand-ing in the peanut butter aisle with no one to guide you. Weighing close to three hundred pounds (and needing to lose a few of those), would you choose Chubb Corpora-tion, which recently came out with a new peanut butter

guaranteed to make you gain weight while just looking at the jar? Or would you choose Skinny, Incorporated, the new fat-free product that tastes great, has zero calories, and is selling like hotcakes?

The choice is not mysterious. You don't need a stockbroker's opinion. However, if your choice is Chubb Corporation, then our suggestion would be . . . step back, reevaluate, and find a fireproof mattress under which you can bury your money.

These examples are food related; somehow we know you aren't surprised. However, you can make your own analysis by focusing on all of the things you buy regularly, such as gasoline, electricity, clothing, computer software, or automobiles. For example if you go to Dunkin' Donuts every morning for breakfast and the place is packed, maybe you should consider buying

stock in Dunkin' Donuts. In other words, *buy what you know*!

Now that you have an idea about how to start thinking about companies that you want to invest with, let's get acquainted with some terms you need to understand.

Notes

CHAPTER TWO

TRANSLATING "STOCKBROKER LINGO"

Or, If I Buy Shares in Wendy's, Will Dave Name a Hamburger After Me?

No, but you will get common stock as a result of your purchase. When we think of stock, the first thing that usually comes to our minds is chicken stock, beef stock, maybe even livestock. Beginning today, when we hear the word *stock,* we are going to think in terms of common stock.

Owning common stock represents ownership of a company. When you buy stock in a corporation, you become a part owner or *stockholder* (also known as a *shareholder*). You immediately own a part, no matter how small, of every building, piece of office furniture, machinery—whatever that company owns.

Think of McDonald's and its "Golden Arches." By owning shares in McDonald's you in fact own a piece of the arches.

Why would anyone want to sell you a part of their company? Here's an example: One day in June 1965 Mc-

Donald's needed to raise money to build more restaurants. Until then it had been privately held. They decided to sell shares in their company and become a publicly traded company.

You could have bought a share that day in June 1965, when the company first issued their shares, for $22.50. Let's just say you purchased one share that day. Thirty years have gone by, it is now December 1995, and you decide to check on the value of that original $22.50 investment you made in 1965. It grew. In fact had you reinvested your dividends all those years, your original investment would now be worth 372 shares of McDonald's valued at $16,830. You can buy a lot of Big Mac's with $16,000!

Does the company itself benefit from the rise in the stock? Not directly. A company *only* makes money when new stock is issued. The first time a company's stock is issued, the company is said to be *going public.* The formal name for this process is an *initial public offering.* The initial public offering of McDonald's was in June 1965.

Let's first understand what "going public" means. Let's suppose that Hilda Homemaker makes the most scrumptious brownies in the world. All of her friends and neighbors encourage her to start selling these delectable goodies.

She takes their advice and approaches several local gourmet shops, who place huge orders. Before she knows it, her kitchen is too small and she cannot keep up with the demand.

She realizes, however, that she is undercapitalized and needs money to make her business grow. Instead of going to the bank for a loan, she decides to approach a friend of hers, who happens to be a stockbroker.

To make a long story short, the stockbroker's firm decides to take Hilda's Brownies public—translated: there is an initial public offering, and as a result Hilda no longer owns her business in its entirety because there are shareholders (co-owners) of her brownie business. She still sells her brownies, but ownership of the company is spread among the shareholders.

Let's look at the reasons companies may choose to issue new stock in order to raise money. Take for example a pharmaceutical company that is on the brink of a cure for cancer . . .

The bank will not lend them money, because they think it is not a sure thing and thus a somewhat risky investment. The company needs money for research and development, so they issue stock for sale to the public.

When you buy shares of this stock, you become a partner with the owners. You own a part of this company. The reason you would want to buy these shares is that you believe this company can find a cure for cancer. If you are correct and they do discover a cure for cancer, the value of the company will be greater. If the value of the company increases, your shares could be worth more.

Let's examine another reason why a company might need to raise money. In the 1980s Walt Disney wanted to expand into France.

Rather than approach the bank to secure a loan for the money needed to expand, Disney opted to raise the money by issuing new shares to the public through a newly formed company called EuroDisney. Individuals who believed that Disney would succeed in Europe bought those shares. Planet Hollywood is another example.

So as we see, some of the primary reasons companies sell shares is to raise money (also known as *capital*) for research, development, and expansion. In the case of the pharmaceutical company they are raising money for research and development to find a cure for cancer. Disney, McDonald's, Planet Hollywood, and Hilda Homemaker, on the other hand, wanted to expand but needed money. They sold shares of their stock to raise the capital. Some other reasons companies raise money are for the creation of jobs or new products or to pay off debt.

One way for companies to raise this money through offering new shares is with the help of people known as *investment bankers.* This is costly, but necessary in order to raise a large sum of money.

Once these shares have been issued, any future trading will most likely occur on one of the three major stock exchanges, the New York Stock Exchange (NYSE), the American Stock Exchange (ASE), or the NASDAQ (Na-

Planet aligns for stock sale

By Suzy Hagstrom

OF THE SENTINEL STAFF

Planet Hollywood International Inc., the restaurant chain with a movie theme, announced plans Monday to sell stock to the public.

Of $190.5 million the Orlando company hopes to raise from the sale, $130 million would pay its debts. Remaining proceeds would finance construction of restaurant-merchandise stores, according to the company's statement.

Planet Hollywood officials would not comment beyond the statement nor would they specify the number of shares to be sold or the share price. The initial public offering is expected in April.

Last month *USA Today* reported that Planet Hollywood planned to sell a minority stake, ranging from 20 percent to 35 percent, to the public. The newspaper said the $150 million in proceeds would finance future growth.

In September, Planet Hollywood garnered $60 million in a private sale. Stockholders include film stars Whoopi Goldberg, Demi Moore, Arnold Schwarzenegger, Sylvester Stallone and Bruce Willis. British magnate Robert Earl is chief executive officer.

It is uncertain from Monday's announcement whether the public would have majority ownership of Planet Hollywood.

Underwriters of the initial public offering are Bear, Stearns & Co. Inc.; Montgomery Securities; Schroder Wertheim & Co.; and Smith Barney Inc. Those brokerages were closed Monday.

tional Association of Securities Dealer Automated Quotation System).

Okay—by now it's lunchtime and you are in line at your favorite fast-food drive-thru restaurant.

While you're devouring the Big Mac, fries, and a milk shake, let's lighten up and let us fill you in on the inside scoop and the purpose of this book.

Here it is: McDonald's—and other companies—can bypass investment bankers and issue shares *directly to you* through what is called a *Direct Investment Plan.* A Direct Investment Plan (DIP) is a program that allows you to make direct purchases of stock in amounts as little as $10. In addition the profits that companies make

and pay out to you the shareholder, known as dividends, can also be reinvested to buy you more shares of the company.

Get back in the drive-thru line and reward yourself with a hot apple pie because now you can acquire more shares by reinvesting your dividends—not to mention the fact that the apple pie you just purchased will mean more sales for McDonald's, which could mean more profit—translated: McDonald's makes money and so do you (what the heck, allow yourself another milk shake to celebrate).

CHAPTER THREE

NOW LET'S TALK DIVIDENDS!

It's Time for the Company to Reward You.

If you own stock in a company that has had a profitable year, they might reward you with a dividend. We call it the icing on your cake. A *dividend* is a cash payment paid to the shareholder from a company's earnings.

Banks pay dividends, but call it interest.

Bosses pay dividends, but call it bonuses.

Husbands pay dividends, but call it chocolates.

Public companies pay dividends, but they call it dividends.

Let's assume you invest $100 in a savings account at the bank and the bank is willing to pay you 8 percent. At the end of one year your account would be worth $108. You earned $8 in interest on your investment of $100.

Let's say you work for the local health club, and the trend this year is fitness. The company shows a much larger profit than they ever imagined. So at year end your boss rewards you with an unexpected and much-appreciated bonus.

When public companies are profitable, meaning they earn money, they may elect to use this extra cash for re-

search and development or for expansion. Or they may decide to reward you, their faithful shareholder, with a dividend. Developing companies might use most of their earnings to finance future growth, or they might pay a small cash dividend, or none at all.

Dividend payments vary according to the specific stock. Companies that historically pay the highest dividends are utility stocks (mainly water companies and power companies). The government controls how much they can charge for their electricity and water and how much profit they can make. Utility companies are confined to a specific area. The prospect of their growing is solely based on the needs of the community in which they provide service.

Since utility company profits are regulated by government agencies, their growth rate is predictable and generally slower than growth stocks. In order to compensate for lower growth, utility companies offer higher dividends to lure the investor.

Stockholders have little say in the control of a corporation; however, they do participate directly in the corporation's successes and failures. The result of a firm's earnings is shown by the profit earned from holding its common stock.

The stock price will go up if the company is earning money, and a dividend could be paid. On the other hand, if the company is being mismanaged, the product becomes obsolete, or the company is losing money, the stock could go down, and the chances of a dividend being paid would be slim.

Isn't it ironic that we want to be slim yet we want our companies to have *big, fat* profits?

The money a firm has left over after all expenses, such as rent, salaries, phone bills, and so on, have been paid can either be reinvested back into the business for new equipment and research or it can be paid to stockholders as dividends. It is like icing on a cake. If a company does well, the stock goes up. And on top of the stock going up in value, a dividend can be declared. We liken it to the company icing (dividend) your cake (stock).

No set rule exists on how much of its earnings a company must distribute as dividends or how often such a distribution will be made to its shareholders.

Most dividends are paid four times a year, but this is solely dependent upon the board of directors of the com-

pany. The board of directors, by vote, can elect to increase, decrease, or cancel dividends depending on the
company's profitability and future plans. One added
note: As a shareholder you have the right to vote for the
directors annually. You will be sent a proxy (an absentee
ballot) to vote for your directors a few months prior to the
annual meeting of the company.

Now, let's suppose that you are a shareholder in a company that does prosper, and the company decides to pay
dividends.

Can it get any better? Yes.

Many companies now offer Dividend Re-Investment
Plans. Not only do they ice your original cake, but the
plan allows you to buy more cakes with *no money out of
your pocket.*

Let's proceed so that we fully understand how to purchase even more shares (cakes) without money from our
own pockets.

CHAPTER FOUR

OKAY—I HAVE THE CAKE, IT'S BEEN ICED, NOW CAN I EAT IT?

From One Cake to a Baker's Dozen Via DRIPs.

Now that we have learned that dividends may be paid on the stock that we have purchased, should we spend the dividends? Absolutely not.

Rather than taking the dividends in cash, you can use them to buy additional shares of stock. Remember Ben Franklin's saying, "Money makes money, and the money that money makes, makes more money." Nothing exemplifies this quotation more vividly than a Dividend Re-Investment Plan—known as a DRIP.

We will give you an example of how rewarding a DRIP can be. Suppose you purchased one share of Coca-Cola when it had its initial public offering in 1919. The company sold those original shares for $40 each. Let's also suppose you reinvested your dividends from the very beginning.

Well, that one share grew—big time. In fact as of December 1995 that original $40 investment was worth

$3,599,046, or 48,472 shares. On the other hand, had you spent those dividends, your investment would have grown to $171,072, or 2,304 shares of Coca-Cola stock.

As the example shows, reinvesting dividends *pays off*!

What exactly is a Dividend Re-Investment Plan, why do companies offer it, and how do you go about setting up a such a plan?

What Is a Dividend Re-Investment Plan and Why Is It Called a DRIP?

Does it have something to do with my plumbing? No.

A DRIP is a program offered by public corporations that allows you to purchase shares in their company without going through a stockbroker.

Approximately one thousand issuers currently offer some form of DRIP. Since the first DRIP was introduced in the late 1960s, there has been considerable evolution in these plans. The greatest change concerns who is permitted to participate in DRIPs. When DRIPs were first introduced in the sixties, the only way you could participate in the plan was if you already owned shares or worked for the company.

In 1994 the Securities and Exchange Commission (SEC) created a model program, cutting much of the red tape involved and thus making it easier for public corporations to set up Dividend Re-Investment Plans. This program meant a lot less paperwork for companies that want to offer shares directly to the public. Translated: you can buy stock directly from the company rather than buying your shares through a stockbroker.

The model program created an easy vehicle for public corporations to set up and administer the direct-purchase plans. When the SEC introduced the new simplified program in December 1994, more companies jumped on the bandwagon, wanting to offer these plans to the public.

We want to note that the SEC does not permit public corporations to advertise their DRIPs. They are allowed to send you information only upon request.

Why Do Companies Want to Offer a Dividend Re-Investment Plan?

One major reason is to develop shareholder loyalty. The larger the number of shares you own, the larger the percentage you own of the company. Let's say you own *a lot* of shares in your favorite fast-food restaurant chain. Which would you frequent, the restaurant you own or that of the competition? How about filling your car up with gasoline? Would you buy gas from the oil company you own or from its competitor?

If you are a loyal customer, you may not be in such a hurry to sell the stock if it is going down, because the reasons you purchased the stock have not changed. The food is still good, the car still runs, the hamburgers taste no different.

These plans also provide an economical and convenient way to raise money (capital) for research and development, general funding, expansion, and all of the other reasons why companies need to raise money. By offering them directly to you, the companies are able to avoid the high cost of an investment banker, who often charges hefty fees.

How Do You Go About Setting Up a Dividend Re-Investment Plan?

Very easily, and if you have a little patience, we will explain in full detail in the next chapter!

What Happens if You Do Not Have Enough Money for One Share of Stock?

This is one of the many benefits of the dividend reinvestment plan. You will be able to buy both whole and fractional shares of stock with the money you send. For example, let's say the stock you currently want to purchase is selling at $50 a share. Let's suppose that you want to invest $10, which is not enough for one whole share. The benefit of the dividend reinvestment plan allows you to purchase fractional shares. In this case you would purchase $^1/_5$ of a share of the stock. If you choose to send in $75 for this same stock, you could buy one whole share and a fraction of another, or $1^1/_2$ shares of stock.

DRIPs offer the individual investor the opportunity to purchase stock directly through the company. Many times there are none of the fees or costs, such as commissions or exchange or handling fees, that are customarily associated with purchasing the stock through a stockbroker.

To summarize, a Dividend Re-Investment Plan, or DRIP, allows you to purchase stock by dealing directly with the company without the meddling of a stockbroker and the fees associated with using a middleman. It also allows you to reinvest the dividends from shares you currently own into purchasing additional shares of the same company.

Obviously DRIPs offer a painless alternative that allows an individual the opportunity to acquire more shares.

Remember Anne Scheiber. Need we say more?

CHAPTER FIVE

FIRST THINGS FIRST: REQUESTING AN APPLICATION

You Can Have Your Cake and Wall Street Too!

The first step is to request an application and prospectus. Don't go running for the kitchen—this is much easier than it sounds. In fact we've done all the hard work for you because we have written the sample letter for you to follow.

The *prospectus* is a brochure full of information about the DRIP that will help you decide if this is the stock for you.

The *application* is the form you will fill out if you decide you want to buy this stock.

First you will need to decide which company you might want to write to and get more information about. For your convenience we have included in Appendix A the names and addresses of companies currently offering direct-investment plans. Turn to the back of the book and browse, and while you do, think about the following:

Let's say you are at our favorite place, the grocery store,

picking up some goodies. You may notice that many of the products you are purchasing are manufactured by Sara Lee, especially if you love coffee cakes, croissants, danishes, and so on. You have decided that that may be

a company you would like to consider owning. Look on the back of a package and find the address you would write to if you had any suggestions or complaints. (From there the letter will be forwarded to the correct department.)

How else do you go about finding names and addresses of companies that are not included in the list at the back of this book?

Go to your local library and locate the business section, or just ask to see the head librarian and let her guide you to the reference section. If she seems a bit uncooperative or reluctant to help, just pull out a bag of chips and start chomping away. That will get her attention and she will become your best friend. Why? She wants you out of there with those crunchy chips ASAP.

The library will have many reference books. One is the Standard & Poors Directory; it will have an information sheet on every publicly traded company. For your information, the name and address will be located at the bottom of each sheet.

Now to the easy part: writing the letter. Again, you want to write directly to the company so that you can buy stock *straight from them* without any stockbrokers or fees.

Now find a sheet of paper, the back of a brown paper bag, an old sandwich wrapper, or whatever you choose. Now turn the page, where you will find a sample letter that we have included for you to copy.

Begin writing or typing, whichever is easier for you.

Obviously you will need to adjust the letter. Just change the italicized words so that your letter has the name of the company as well as your own name and address.

When you've finished your letter, find an envelope

March 19, 1996

XYZ Corporation
123 State Street
Anywhere, USA 00000

Attn: Shareholder Relations

Dear Sir or Madam:

Please send me a copy of the prospectus and application for your Dividend Re-Investment Plan:
      Your Name
      Your Address
      Your City, State, and Zip Code

Thank you for your attention to this matter.

Sincerely,

Your Name

(nothing fancy) and write the same addresses there. Now
you've really earned a treat!

In the letter you have just written you have requested
that the company send you an application (for you to
complete if you choose to purchase this company's
stock) and a prospectus. A prospectus is sent for two
reasons.

First, it is a requirement that must be satisfied in order
to comply with the laws of the Securities and Exchange
Commission. Second, the prospectus, on which we'll go

into detail later, is considered to be your owner's manual that explains how the Dividend Re-Investment Plan works.

Even though you have requested this application for yourself, it does not mean you are required to purchase this stock or are in any way indebted to this company! This is just a request to obtain the information, and then you decide whether or not you want to consider this Dividend Re-Investment Plan for yourself, your uncle, your child, your next-door neighbor, or whomever.

Once the letter has been written, you can expect the application and prospectus to be mailed to you within seven to ten working days. We suggest you get some manila file folders and label them with the name of each of the companies from which you have requested applications. This will help you keep organized and will offer easy access when you want to verify information about the plan.

Now it's time just to sit by your mailbox and wait.

Notes

CHAPTER SIX

THE COMPANY ACTUALLY SENT ME THE PROSPECTUS AND APPLICATION!

The Prospectus Isn't on the Best-seller List. . . . Do I Really Have to Read It?

Absolutely! So get into your favorite easy chair, relax, and enjoy reading the prospectus—in fact you may discover it beats a lot of the books that are on the best-seller list. (Okay, so that's a stretch, but we're trying to entice you to read it, because it contains many things you will need to know.)

A prospectus describes an offering to a potential buyer. The cover page of every prospectus will state the following:

These securities have not been approved or disapproved by the Securities and Exchange Commission or any State Securities Commission nor has the Securities and Exchange Commission passed upon the accuracy or adequacy of this prospectus. Any representation to the contrary is a criminal offense.

PROSPECTUS

McCORMICK & COMPANY, INCORPORATED

200,000 Shares of Common Stock
200,000 Shares of Common Stock Non-Voting

McCORMICK DIVIDEND REINVESTMENT PLAN

The Dividend Reinvestment Plan, as amended (the "Plan") of McCormick & Company, Incorporated (the "Company") provides each registered holder of the Company's Common Stock and Common Stock Non-Voting with a simple and convenient method of reinvesting cash dividends and making optional cash investments in additional shares of the same class of common stock.

The original Dividend Reinvestment Plan, which was explained in a Registration Statement filed with the Securities and Exchange Commission on March 11, 1983, Registration No. 2-82375, was amended on December 18, 1989 and has subsequently been amended as follows: (i) the requirement that the optional cash investment not exceed the amount of the dividend has been eliminated but the minimum ($100) and maximum ($3,000) quarterly investment limitations have been maintained, (ii) new month end deadlines for the receipt of Authorization Cards for enrollment in the Plan, for making changes to investment options and for sending optional cash payments to the Company have been established, and (iii) Plan participants now have the option of designating either a percentage or a number of shares of Common Stock and/or Common Stock Non-Voting for partial dividend reinvestment. This amendment is effective on the date appearing at the bottom of page one of this Prospectus.

On November 20, 1989 and November 19, 1991, the Company announced a 2 for 1 split of both classes of its common stock. The stock splits were effected by distribution on January 19, 1990 and January 17, 1992 of certificates of one new share for each share held of record at the close of business on December 29, 1989 and December 31, 1991. The number of shares recited as being offered pursuant to this Prospectus has not been adjusted for either of these splits.

Participants in the Plan may acquire additional shares of the Company's Common Stock and Common Stock Non-Voting by:

(i) reinvesting all of their cash dividends (less any required federal income tax withholding), or reinvesting any part of their cash dividends and continuing to receive a check for the balance; and

(ii) making optional cash investments in additional shares of the same class of the Company's common stock as the shares for which the participant has elected dividend reinvestment, for any dividend payment date, in an amount not less than $100 but not greater than $3,000, per class of stock.

Shares of Common Stock and Common Stock Non-Voting acquired by participants in the Plan will consist of original issue shares sold to participants by the Company, or shares purchased on the open market by an independent agent or agents. The methods for determining the prices of such shares are set forth in the answer to Question 14 contained on page 8 of this Prospectus. You may enroll in the Plan by completing an Authorization Card and returning it to the Company. Authorization Cards may be obtained from the Company. This Prospectus relates to shares of Common Stock and Common Stock Non-Voting of the Company registered for purchase under the Plan.

The date of this Prospectus is November 23, 1992.

The Securities and Exchange Commission is to the securities industry what the Food and Drug Administration (FDA) is to food. For example, while the FDA does not guarantee the taste of a certain cereal, it does demand that the ingredients be disclosed to the consumer. Once again, the decision is up to you.

The opening statement of the prospectus gives an overview of the shareholder investment plan. It tells you how the dividends are reinvested, who the administrator is, and the number of shares that can be sold under this prospectus. Each of these items is explained in detail within the prospectus.

Let's take for example the table of contents from McCormick & Company, and go over each item. Remember, every item in this prospectus will also be covered in any other prospectus that you request. It may have a different title, but flour is flour whether it is Gold Medal or Pillsbury.

☞ *Available Information*—All companies are required to file with the Securities and Exchange Commission a Registration Statement. This information will include the company's annual report and each of their quarterly reports. But, if you have a hard time balancing your own checkbook, then these will be reports that you will *not* want to request from the company. However, once you become a shareholder, the company will send you these reports.

☞ *Information Incorporated by Reference*—This gives a list of documents that can be found in the Public Reference Room at the SEC in Washington, D.C. No, don't start making airline reservations—you don't have to make the trip. In fact if you have trouble bal-

TABLE OF CONTENTS

ancing your checkbook, don't bother visiting the Public Reference Room even if you happen to live in Washington!

☞ *The Company*—This part is reminiscent of our children's birth certificates. It tells where and when the company was born.

☞ *Use of Proceeds*—When companies are issuing new shares through their Dividend Re-Investment Plan, all of the proceeds from the sale of the stock will go directly to the company. The prospectus will spell out for you what the company plans to do with the money that it raises. Most of the time they will be using these proceeds for general corporate purposes. Okay, let's not be totally unrealistic. We are not just talking Scotch tape, staples, and office furniture. It may also include a few $500 lunches and a couple of trips to Tahiti, but this all goes under the heading of expenses, because it has an impact on the daily working operations of the corporation and usually shows up on the profit-and-loss statement as a travel and entertainment expense.

☞ *Description of Dividend Re-Investment Plan*—This is the highlight—all the nitty-gritty details of how we go from barely affording a bicycle to riding in a limo! This section will detail any costs incurred as a result of your reinvesting dividends, purchasing additional shares, and selling shares.

This is the most important area to us. We are choosing not to use stockbrokers because of the fees and commissions. We want to make every penny work for us. So pay careful attention to this section. Now that we are doing it on our own, let's try not to incur any unnecessary costs. Sometimes plans may have fees. It is *very important* that we be aware of the fees and determine if it is wise that we pay them to purchase this stock or if we would be better off investing with another company. We want *all* of our money to work for us.

This section will also tell who is eligible to participate in the plan. It may be necessary that you own shares (it can be as little as one share) in the company before you can participate in the Dividend Re-Investment Plan. If that is the case, you must buy the initial share(s) through a stockbroker. Call a local stockbrokerage firm, preferably a discount firm, and ask what the total fees and commission would be if you were to purchase X number of shares as well as have the stock delivered to you. You want to make sure that the stock certificate is sent to you by mail and is registered in the name you requested (whether it be your name, your sister's name, or your child's name) so that you can set up your Dividend Re-Investment Plan directly through the company. If your shares are held by the brokerage firm, your stock company will not know that you own shares in their company and you will not be able to set up a Dividend Re-Investment Plan.

If the fees are acceptable to you, go for it; if not, call another brokerage firm and shop around till you feel comfortable with the fees.

This section also goes over the different options

you have when the dividends are paid, such as: do you want full dividend reinvestment (where all the dividends are reinvested to purchase more shares), or do you want a partial dividend reinvestment (where half of your money is reinvested in more shares and the other half of the dividend is sent to you). It is time that we repeat what our old friend Ben said: "Money makes money, and the money that money makes, makes more money." In other words you are going to want to reinvest *all* your dividends.

This area will also talk about optional cash investment. Some companies have no minimum; it could be a $10 a month minimum or it could be $1,000 a month. The prospectus will also include the maximum that one can contribute. Some companies have been very generous and will allow you to contribute up to $60,000 or more during a quarter. We will reiterate, these are *optional* cash payments, and you do not have to make them.

We strongly encourage you to commit to a systematic plan where you will comfortably contribute a fixed dollar amount on a fixed day, be it weekly or monthly, over a fixed time period. This is called *dollar cost averaging.* Now, don't panic—if you need a little snack to relax yourself over those fancy words, fine. We will explain dollar cost averaging later. And be assured, we will make the concept easier than riding a bicycle! Guaranteed!

Finally, this section discusses the day on which shares will be purchased for your plan.

☞ *Termination of Plan Participation*—This section will discuss how you go about getting your money when you no longer want to participate in the plan. You can reasonably expect your money to be returned to you within ten days.

☞ *Reports to Participants*—This section will explain that you will receive quarterly statements reflecting all activity in your account. If you have sent in money, you will want to check and make sure that your account has been properly credited.

☞ *Tax Consequences*—Dividends are taxable, just like the interest earned on savings accounts or other investments you may have. You will receive the necessary papers from the company in order to file your tax returns by January 31 of each year.

☞ *Other Information*—This includes bits of information that you may or may not find useful. Sometimes

they will talk about stock splits, annual meetings, who is administrating the plan, and so forth.

☞ *Legal Matters*—This part tells who the attorneys are that represent your company. There will probably be so many people listed in the name of the firm that it will fill the page! But then again, it can feel impressive and comforting since in essence they are now working for you.

☞ *Experts*—Also known as the CPAs that represent the company. They work for you, too, if you are a shareholder. Feeling pretty important now? Then let's move forward while we're still on a roll!

Notes

CHAPTER SEVEN

I STUMBLED THROUGH THE PROSPECTUS—NOW, WHAT IS THIS?

The Application—And We Don't Mean for Another Charge Card!

Nobody can do just one! No, we're not talking potato chips—we're referring to the application or enrollment form. We know you can be intimidated by this, but let us set you at ease. The majority of enrollment forms all request the same basic information; in fact they request less than is required to apply for a charge card from your local department store.

Believe it or not, it's so easy that you'll be able to complete your first application in less time than it takes to finish a bag of chips!

On the following page is an application that we will work with throughout this chapter to illustrate our examples.

The first item on the form asks the amount you wish to invest. If you plan on filling in $20 million, stop reading the book at this point. For the rest of you who will not be

filling in $20 million in that little box, you need to keep on reading!

Below the square box is the minimum amount of dollars needed to open this account. Some direct-investment plans will have no minimum, while others could have an initial investment as low as $50 or even $10. The only way to determine the required minimum of the initial investment is to read the prospectus.

The second item deals with account registration. Every form we have ever seen explains in detail the different types of ownership. We have itemized below the most common registrations:

GETTING RICH ON JUST $10 A WEEK !

INVESTOR SERVICES PLAN

APPLICATION FORM

IMPORTANT

Return this application together with your check in the enclosed envelope or send to:

TEXACO INC.
P.O. Box 10818
Newark, NJ 07193-0818

PLEASE **PRINT** CLEARLY

Citizenship: ☐ U.S.   ☐ Foreign

MAKE CHECK PAYABLE TO:

TEXACO INC.

AMOUNT OF INVESTMENT

1

($250 MINIMUM - $120,000 MAXIMUM)

**SOCIAL SECURITY NO.
(TAXPAYER I.D. NUMBER)**

4

(OF ACCOUNT TO BE OPENED)

<u>ACCOUNT REGISTRATION</u> (See Information on Reverse Side)

NAME (1)

NAME (2) (If applicable)

NAME (3) (If applicable)

STREET ADDRESS (P.O. BOX)

CITY   STATE   ZIP CODE

3 DIVIDEND REINVESTMENT

Participants must select either 100% or 0% (zero percent) dividend reinvestment.

Please check the appropriate box.

☐ 100% Dividend Reinvestment

☐ 0% (Zero Percent) Dividend Reinvestment

NOTE: If you are registering a living trust, the above registration must include the name of the trustee(s) and date of the trust agreement.

GIFTING

Does this enrollment represent a gift to a third party?   ☐ Yes   ☐ No

If you answered yes, please indicate the complete address of the individual to whom you wish the gift certificate to be sent. If you do not provide an address in the space below, the gift certificate will be mailed directly to the first party indicated above.

NAME

STREET ADDRESS (P.O. BOX)

CITY   STATE   ZIP CODE

ACKNOWLEDGEMENTS AND AUTHORIZATIONS

I acknowledge receipt of the prospectus describing the details of the Investor Services Plan (the "Plan") and hereby request that the above account be enrolled in the Plan. Enclosed is a check or money order for the amount indicated above to be applied toward the purchase of shares for the above account. I understand that the account's participation is subject to the Terms and Conditions of the Plan as set forth in the prospectus that accompanied this Application Form, and that enrollment may be discontinued at any time by written notice to Texaco Inc., Investor Services Plan, 2000 Westchester Ave., White Plains, New York 10650.

I further understand that all dividends paid on the shares held in the account will be automatically reinvested unless I select the 0% (zero percent) dividend reinvestment option. I hereby appoint Texaco Inc. as agent for applying dividends as payment for any such shares purchased for the above account under the Plan.

Under penalties of perjury, I certify that the Social Security Number (Taxpayer Identification Number) indicated above is true and correct and that I am not subject to back-up withholding per the Internal Revenue Code. Please note that if a Social Security Number (Taxpayer Identification Number) is not provided, back-up withholding tax will be withheld from dividend payments.

Signed _____ Date _____

OTHER INFORMATION

Please provide daytime telephone number where you may be contacted in the event additional information is required: (_____)_____

☞ *Individual*—A person who owns property solely in his or her name only.

☞ *Joint Tenancy*—Two or more owners have an equal interest in the stock. If one person dies, the other person automatically receives the interest of the deceased owner. Examples of registration on a joint account: a husband and wife, Mr. and Mrs. John Doe; or two sisters, Mrs. Mary Smith and Mrs. Jane Doe.

☞ *Custodian Account*—If you plan to purchase shares for a minor (anyone under the age of eighteen), it is necessary to open a custodian account. In setting up the custodian account, you would use the child's Social Security number. When the child comes of age, all that is necessary is for her to provide a birth certificate to the company to show she is the legal owner of the stock.

☞ *Trust Account*—The account should be titled the same as the trust, which is a legal document prepared by your attorney.

☞ *IRA*—Some Dividend Re-Investment Plans will allow you to open an IRA directly through them rather than going through a stockbrokerage firm or bank. Remember, the prospectus will contain the information needed about IRAs (that's why it's required reading).

★The third item asks what you want to do with the dividends. We are not talking shopping binges or European vacations here. As Ben Franklin said, "Money makes money, and the money that money makes, makes more money."

We highly recommend that you reinvest 100 percent of your dividends.

★The fourth item—Social Security number. All citizens two months of age and older are now required by the United States government to have a Social Security number. This section requires that you not only have your Social Security number on file, but that you give written certification as to its correctness.

CHAPTER EIGHT

FORGET THE BICYCLE— I'M ON MY WAY TO AFFORDING A LIMO

Now, How Do I Operate It?
Or, Interpreting Your Statement.

We all know that once we learn to ride a bicycle, we never forget. Well, it's the same with learning how to operate a limo—except that you have to start with the owner's manual, in this case the statement.

So let us teach you how to read a statement that will be similar to the one you will receive once you become a shareholder.

It's a piece of cake! Thereafter every time you get your statement, it will be as easy to read as riding that old discarded bicycle.

On page 73 is a sample of a Dividend Re-Investment Plan for Exxon Corporation, which we will use to explain each item throughout this chapter.

A. *Account Number*—This is your own personal account number. No two accounts will ever have the

same number. It is always a good idea to reference your account number on your check as well as on any correspondence. Your account number is similar to a Social Security number—only one person in the world will have it, and it will coincide with the account registration.

B. *Account Registration*—This information is obtained from the application that you completed. Make sure of the correct spelling of your name and address when you receive your first statement to avoid any future problems.

C. *Tax ID Number*—Also known as your Social Security number.

D. *Current Dividend Option*—You are usually given one of three options:

1. *Full Dividend Re-Investment*—All of your dividends paid will be used to purchase additional shares of stock. YES! This is our choice.

2. *Partial Dividend Re-Investment*—Half of the dividends that are paid on your shares will be sent to you, and the other half will be used to purchase additional shares.

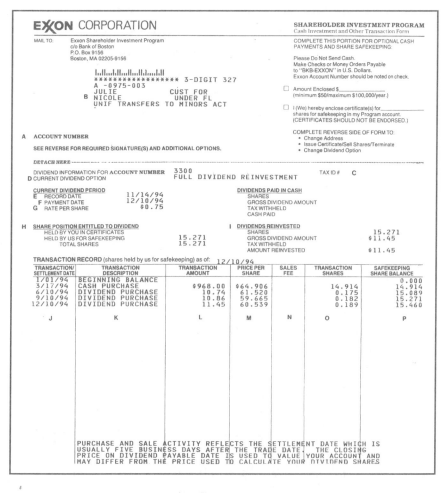

EXXON CORPORATION

SHAREHOLDER INVESTMENT PROGRAM
Cash Investment and Other Transaction Form

MAIL TO: Exxon Shareholder Investment Program
c/o Bank of Boston
P.O. Box 9156
Boston, MA 02205-9156

COMPLETE THIS PORTION FOR OPTIONAL CASH
PAYMENTS AND SHARE SAFEKEEPING:

Please Do Not Send Cash.
Make Checks or Money Orders Payable
to "BKB-EXXON" in U.S. Dollars.
Exxon Account Number should be noted on check.

****************** 3-DIGIT 327
A -0975-003
JULIE   CUST FOR
NICOLE   UNDER FL
UNIF TRANSFERS TO MINORS ACT

☐ Amount Enclosed $_____
(minimum $50/maximum $100,000/year.)

☐ I (We) hereby enclose certificate(s) for_____
shares for safekeeping in my Program account.
(CERTIFICATES SHOULD NOT BE ENDORSED.)

A ACCOUNT NUMBER

SEE REVERSE FOR REQUIRED SIGNATURE(S) AND ADDITIONAL OPTIONS.

COMPLETE REVERSE SIDE OF FORM TO:
• Change Address
• Issue Certificate/Sell Shares/Terminate
• Change Dividend Option

DETACH HERE

DIVIDEND INFORMATION FOR ACCOUNT NUMBER   3300
D CURRENT DIVIDEND OPTION   FULL DIVIDEND REINVESTMENT   TAX ID #   **C**

CURRENT DIVIDEND PERIOD
E RECORD DATE   11/14/94
F PAYMENT DATE   12/10/94
G RATE PER SHARE $0.75

DIVIDENDS PAID IN CASH
SHARES
GROSS DIVIDEND AMOUNT
TAX WITHHELD
CASH PAID

H SHARE POSITION ENTITLED TO DIVIDEND
HELD BY YOU IN CERTIFICATES
HELD BY US FOR SAFEKEEPING   15.271
TOTAL SHARES   15.271

I DIVIDENDS REINVESTED
SHARES   15.271
GROSS DIVIDEND AMOUNT $11.45
TAX WITHHELD
AMOUNT REINVESTED $11.45

TRANSACTION RECORD (shares held by us for safekeeping) as of: 12/10/94

TRANSACTION/ SETTLEMENT DATE	TRANSACTION DESCRIPTION	TRANSACTION AMOUNT	PRICE PER SHARE	SALES FEE	TRANSACTION SHARES	SAFEKEEPING SHARE BALANCE
1/01/94	BEGINNING BALANCE					0.000
3/17/94	CASH PURCHASE	$968.00	$64.906		14.914	14.914
6/10/94	DIVIDEND PURCHASE	10.74	61.520		0.175	15.089
9/10/94	DIVIDEND PURCHASE	10.86	59.665		0.182	15.271
12/10/94	DIVIDEND PURCHASE	11.45	60.539		0.189	15.460
J	**K**	**L**	**M**	**N**	**O**	**P**

PURCHASE AND SALE ACTIVITY REFLECTS THE SETTLEMENT DATE WHICH IS
USUALLY FIVE BUSINESS DAYS AFTER THE TRADE DATE. THE CLOSING
PRICE ON DIVIDEND PAYABLE DATE IS USED TO VALUE YOUR ACCOUNT AND
MAY DIFFER FROM THE PRICE USED TO CALCULATE YOUR DIVIDEND SHARES.

3. *No Re-Investment*—This is a no-no if you want to be riding in that limo.

E. *Record Date*—The day a stockholder must be carried on the company's books in order to receive the dividend. If you purchase shares too late to appear on the firm's books, that is to say, after the record date, you will not receive the dividend on the current payment date.

F. *Payment Date*—The day dividend checks are sent to stockholders by the corporation's banks—or the day your dividend is reinvested in more shares of stock. Once you have discovered the approximate date that dividends are reinvested for you, you should declare that day an official holiday. You are now officially participating in a DRIP—and this offers a whole new reason to celebrate!

G. *Rate per Share*—The amount of dividend paid per share. In this example, for every share you own you will receive $0.75. If you own one-half of one share, you will receive one-half of the amount, or $0.375.

H. *Share Position Entitled to Dividend*—You may have been given shares of stock or actually purchased shares in the past and were issued a certificate. Unless they are held by the company, they are considered to be in certificate form. If you own shares of stock, and the stock is being held by your stockbroker, they will be in *street name.*

Which means, stock is not held in a certificate by your stockbroker stating that you own ten shares, or John Jones owns four shares, or Niki Noodle owns seven shares, etc. Your shares are merely a back-office transaction within the brokerage house (this does not mean that it is not yours, merely that it is held by the brokerage firm) and the company you have purchased does not know you own shares in their company.

Translated, if your shares are in street name at your brokerage firm, your shares are commingled with all the other clients of the firm, all over the world.

Let's give you an example. You have a checking account at the local bank and you have deposited your paycheck. Your money is commingled with that of all the other bank customers. The bank does not have a separate cubbyhole for your money nor for anyone else's. When you pay your bills, the bank clerk does not go to your cubby and withdraw your money to cover your check. However, you do have an account, in which a record is kept of your deposits and withdrawals. It works the same with your shares that are being held at the brokerage firm.

Let's say you have decided to set up a DRIP. You must have those shares delivered to you or placed in safekeeping at the stockbrokerage firm so that the company will know you own the stock.

Another reason for having your stock registered in your own name is so that the company knows you are a shareholder. They may want to share some freebies with you. Our children own the Wrigley Corporation, and every Christmas they send them a twenty-pack carton of chewing gum. Had the stock been in street name at the stockbrokerage firm, Wrigley would not know our children were the stock's owners and they would not have sent them any chewing gum.

I. *Dividends Re-invested*—Exxon Corporation is going to pay $0.75 on 15.271 shares, or $11.45.

J. *Transaction/Settlement Date*—The day on which money is deposited, dividends are paid, or any other activity occurs in your account.

K. *Transaction Description*—This reflects all the activity that takes place in your account.

L. *Transaction Amount*—The total number of dollars that are involved because of the transaction. If you sent them a check for $28, make sure that $28 is reflected in this column.

M. *Price per Share*—The price of the stock on the day your purchase of additional shares was made.

N. *Sales Fee*—Check the prospectus and see why and when fees will be charged. The reason we are participating in DRIPs is to keep our costs down. If the sales fees are high, shouldn't you reconsider this particular company?

O. *Transaction Shares*—The number of shares that are purchased. You will note that even though you may not have enough money for a whole share, the company will buy fractional shares for you. This is great for those of us who cannot afford to purchase whole shares!

P. *Safekeeping Share Balance*—This is a running total of the total number of shares you own.

Finally, here are a few further points you should be aware of:

☞ The statement is a reflection of all the activity in your account.

☞ The statement should be reviewed when received and could be treated as a bill—that is, when the statement comes in, review it, then forward the company more money to buy more shares.

☞ For tax purposes, it is only important that you save the year-end statement, because that will reflect all of the activity that transpired during the year.

CHAPTER NINE

READING THE STOCK TABLE CAN BE AS EASY AS OPENING A BOX OF CEREAL

As soon as you become a stockholder, breakfast might take on a whole new meaning: You will rush to review the stock table before you even begin to think about breakfast, your commute time, or your car pool. Once you are an investor, you will find it hard to resist the business section of your local newspaper.

But *beware*—just as you are told not to jump on the scale every morning when you're on a diet, we advise that you refrain from monitoring the price fluctuation of your·stock on a daily basis.

It can be hazardous to your attitude and can play havoc with your day if your stock is not moving up on a steady basis. Remember, you are in this for the long haul, and day-to-day price movement does not reflect the big picture.

You must also realize that stocks are traded in multi-

ples of one eighth of a point. A point is equal to one dollar. So a one-eighth-point price increase or decrease is equivalent to a difference of $0.125, or 12½ cents per share.

Granted 12½ cents per share may seem like very little

if your stock is going up, but it can represent a lot more in mental fatigue if your stock is falling! Do yourself a favor and don't follow your stock so closely. You will be happier, and your friends and family will still like to be around you.

Now, to help you with those mornings when you feel compelled to know what your stock is doing, we have clipped a line out of our local newspaper.

52 Weeks			Sym	Yld Div	%	PE	Vol 100s	Hi	Lo	Close	Net Chg
Hi	Lo	Stock									
86	68^1/$_8$	Exxon	XON	3.00	3.6	16	18707	85^1/$_4$	83^3/$_4$	84^1/$_4$	—^{3}/$_8$

Translated, it goes like this.

52 Weeks

HI	LO
86	68^1/$_8$

The stock we are using in our example is Exxon Corporation. During the previous fifty-two weeks, Exxon traded as high as 86 per share and as low as 68^1/$_8$. As we have explained, stocks trade in denominations of one eighth, which is equivalent to 12^1/$_2$ cents per share. Translated: the high on Exxon was $86.00 and the low was $68.125 per share, or 68 dollars and 12^1/$_2$ cents.

Stock
Exxon

This is the name of the stock you are following. Stocks are listed in the newspaper alphabetically and might be abbreviated in some form or another.

Sym
XON

This is known as the symbol or ticker symbol. If you are sitting home one afternoon with nothing to do, turn on the financial news network on your local TV. On the screen below the commentators is a ticker tape with lots of mixed-up letters just like the one that you have been seeing at the top of all the pages in this book. So now you know that (a) your eyes weren't playing tricks; (b) you still know how to read; and (c) you aren't dyslexic.

Div
3.00

Remember the icing on the cake. The dividend amount of $3 is the amount of cash paid for each share of stock owned in Exxon [over the previous twelve months]. Dividends are normally paid every three months.

Yld
%
3.6

This is the yield on Exxon. Yield is the rate of return on your investment. To determine the yield, you would divide the dividend, in this case $3, by the price per share, assuming you purchased the stock at 84¼. The yield would be 3.6 percent.

PE
16

PE is an abbreviation for price-earnings ratio. The ratio is determined by dividing the company's stock price by the company's earnings. Don't get your calculator out. The newspaper will have done calculations for you. In our example the number 16 was derived by dividing the price of the stock by the company's earnings. Many serious investors study the price earnings of a particular stock or industry. The price-earnings ratio will vary between industries. The food industry may have an average of 10, while the drug industry may have an average of 32.

The investment gurus say that in today's market the average stock has a PE of 16—and who are we to argue with the gurus?

Don't think in terms of a PE being good or bad if it's high or low. The PE is *one of many* tools used by professional portfolio managers as well as stockbrokers as a measure of the stock price in relationship to its earnings.

As we stressed in previous chapters, this is *only one of* many tools that a stockbroker may consider in his evaluation of a stock. Certainly mothers every day plan menus for their families without the help of a dietitian, therefore why can an individual not make choices in other areas of their life—i.e., purchasing stock. In basic language, *buy what you know*!

In other words, when you buy a box of cereal, do you check how much riboflavin is in it? Probably not, but a dietitian would.

Vol
100s
18707

Volume is the number of shares that have been traded on that day. Let's look at our example. The figure that is quoted is 18,707, but the newspapers abbreviate it to save space. You should always add two zeros to the figure to determine the total shares traded. If you are mathematically inclined, multiply 18,707 by 100. So the true amount traded on the New York Stock Exchange is 1,870,700 shares for that day.

Hi

$85^{1}/_{4}$

During the day, stock prices will fluctuate in value. On this particular day the high for Exxon was $85^{1}/_{4}$ per share.

Lo

$83^{3}/_{4}$

The lowest the stock traded at during the day was $83^{3}/_{4}$. In dollars and cents that would be equivalent of $83.75. Remember, stocks trade in increments of one eighth of a point, or $12^{1}/_{2}$ cents per share.

Obviously your next question is why does it trade at different prices throughout the day? The reason stocks fluctuate is because of supply and demand.

Here is an example: A grandmother in Seattle, Washington, decides to purchase a big block of stock for her granddaughter's birthday. She needs it today, so she places her order to buy the shares with her stockbroker.

Across the country in Orlando, Florida, a young couple need money for a down payment on their first home. They need to sell their stock, which they received as a wedding gift three years ago. They called their stockbroker and told him to sell their stock. These orders are then executed on the New York Stock Exchange.

Let's suppose that there are two hundred grandmothers buying the same stock on the same day—it would create a *demand* for the stock, thereby causing prices to *move up.*

On the other hand, if two hundred young couples were to sell their stock on the same day, it would create a *supply,* causing the price to *go down.*

These examples are just two of the kinds of things that go on all day long on the New York Stock Exchange. In our example Exxon traded over one million shares. That is a lot of grandmas buying, but that is also a lot of people selling. The last trade of the day would be the last price the stock traded at on that day, or the closing price.

Close
$84^{1}/_{4}$

The stock closed at $84^{1}/_{4}$ that day.

Net Chg
$-^{3}/_{8}$

It was down three eighths of a point from the previous day. Remember three eighths of a point equals $37^{1}/_{2}$ cents per share. If you owned one hundred shares, that would mean $37.50. Don't panic, you're in for the long haul!

CHAPTER TEN

DOLLAR COST AVERAGING

What Is This . . . Metric Conversion?

No, it's much easier than that. Let's look at a very simple buying program that will ensure that years from now you are still buying cakes (stocks). Don't raid the refrigerator; this concept is painless and easy to digest. First, commit to investing a fixed amount of money at a fixed interval. How can you do that?

If you always eat pizza on Friday night and spend $20, compromise and take $10 and buy pizza and the other $10 and buy stock.

This has an added benefit for those of us constantly battling the bulge. If you buy a smaller pizza, it means fewer calories. Not realistic? Maybe not, since the invention of stuffed crust, but since we all want to be able to afford a pizza twenty years from now, it could be a good compromise.

Dollar cost averaging is a tried-and-true recipe. The ac-

tual dollar amount invested is not as important as establishing a set time each month to invest your money (whether shares are going up or down in price). In other words *consistent investing,* rather than the actual dollar amount invested, is the critical factor.

When purchasing stock directly from the company, it is common to find different minimum investment requirements. Some stocks set minimal initial and subsequent investments as low as $10, some $25, and some even $100. You must set realistic goals for yourself and you must read the prospectus to determine the amount of your initial purchase and all future deposits.

When investing, always keep in mind that investment return and principal value will fluctuate due to market conditions. But by instituting the dollar-cost-averaging method to investing, you will always be buying the most stock when prices are low and the least number of shares when prices are high.

For example, if you were investing $100 a month and the stock was trading at $20 per share, you would purchase five new shares of stock. What if the stock dropped to $10? Time to panic and binge on your favorite snack? NO! Celebrate, because you are now able to purchase ten new shares of stock at a lower cost. When the stock was trading $20 a share, you were only able to purchase five shares.

We have learned that stock prices can fluctuate on a daily basis. Therefore by consistently purchasing your shares at the same time each month with the same amount of money, the price per share that you will pay will average out over the years.

On the following page is a chart that shows the amount of shares acquired by one individual in a Dividend Re-Investment Plan. As you can see, the second column represents the amount of money invested each month over a period of sixteen months.

The third column shows the price at which the stock was purchased during that month. And the fourth column reflects the number of shares you were able to acquire with your $25.

Month	Monthly Investment	Price per Share	Number of Shares Purchased
JAN	25.00	10.00	2.50
FEB	25.00	9.00	2.77
MAR	25.00	8.00	3.13
APR	25.00	7.00	3.57
MAY	25.00	6.00	4.33
JUN	25.00	5.00	5.00
JUL	25.00	4.00	6.25
AUG	25.00	3.00	8.33
SEPT	25.00	2.00	12.50
OCT	25.00	1.00*	25.00
NOV	25.00	2.00	12.50
DEC	25.00	3.00	8.33
JAN	25.00	4.00	6.25
FEB	25.00	5.00	5.00
MAR	25.00	6.00	4.33
APR	25.00	7.00	3.57
	Total Investment: $400.00	Closing Stock Price: $7.00	Total Number of Shares Owned: 113.36

*Wow! My $25 bought twenty-five shares in October!

Immediately you see that the month after you invested your initial $25, the stock started going down in price, in fact to as low as one dollar a share.

However, as you will note, eventually the stock price began to rebound and started to go back up. By now you are saying, "I bought the original stock at $10, and after sixteen months each share is worth *only* $7." Relax, remember, we are holding on to the stock as a *long-term in-*

vestment, not an instant "get rich quick" vehicle. Don't panic, as this is where the beauty of dollar cost averaging enters the picture.

At the end of sixteen months your total investment of $400.00 is worth $793.52 (this figure is reached by multiplying the total number of shares purchased (113.36) by the last price ($7) to determine the current value of your $25-a-month investment over this period of time.

Dollar cost averaging, which simply means investing the same amount of money at a fixed interval (weekly, monthly, etc.) is hardly a new technique. It cannot assure a profit or protect against a loss. But using dollar cost averaging, you will develop the discipline needed to establish a successful long-term financial plan.

CHAPTER ELEVEN

START INVESTING TODAY— WITHOUT DELAY!

You Now Have All the Knowledge You Need to Become a Shareholder.

Oops! Did we forget to mention that we expect each and every one of you who has read this book to send us a picture of you in your limo? And for those of you who don't particularly want a limo, then of course we will lovingly accept huge boxes of goodies (i.e., cake, pies, danishes, brownies, pastries, etc.). Oh, and we both love jewelry, so that's quite acceptable as well! Seriously, we hope that with this book we have given you the necessary information you need to begin to secure your financial future. That was our sincere reason for taking on this challenge. (Plus it gave us the added benefit of losing a few pounds, because we didn't have as much time to eat!)

You probably now have forty-seven questions. Let us answer a couple that we know you might have:

☞ *How many companies should I purchase?*

Whatever number you feel comfortable with. We cannot tell you four is better than seven. What we can say is that when you begin, it is very important to be consistent with the same number of dollars invested in the same time frame, be it weekly, monthly, or quarterly.

☞ *Should I buy all oil stocks or only Georgia Utility companies?*

No, it is best to diversify. You would not want to own seven houses on the same block in the same city, unless of course it was Rodeo Drive. Anything more than one is diversification. Again, our motto is: When you begin, it is very important to be consistent with the same number of dollars invested in the same time frame.

Mutual funds are the most publicized investment in the financial world and they are a perfect example of diversification.

A mutual fund is a portfolio of stocks. Let us give you an example.

Assume you are shopping at the grocery store, you are in the dairy aisle, and you load into your shopping basket only dairy products, such as milk, cottage cheese, sour cream, butter, and so on. In the mutual-fund industry they would call this a mutual fund that specializes in the dairy industry.

You decide instead that you want to add a little meat, vegetables, and fruit. This would be called a diversified basket, or a diversified mutual fund.

If you feel you are not informed enough to create your own basket of goodies, request the prospectus from any mutual fund and see what stocks they are buying! You can mimic their choices if you're still feeling a little less than confident about your own ability to choose stocks.

☞ *When do I sell my stock?*

When the reasons that you originally purchased the stock have changed. What this means, for example is the following: You purchased Coca-Cola Company because that is the only soft drink your family would consume. Years go by, your family has decided that Pepsi has a much better taste, it has new products that you like, and the price is much lower. If you were investing today based on your family's feelings, would you still purchase Coca-Cola?

Now you're feeling, "I can handle this. Where to now?" In Appendix B we have listed some additional suggested readings that will help expand your knowledge.

It is never too late to start. It is a fact of life that we are all growing older each day (even those of you who look like Elle Macpherson or Brad Pitt—your time is coming).

So when we start to lose our hair or we color it enough to be referred to as a blue-hair, when it's hard to remember where our waistline used to be, when those varicose veins start crying out for support hose and maybe you aren't brushing teeth that are permanently attached to your gums, at least you will have the money you need to live graciously. (And let's not forget that living graciously may require the help of a plastic surgeon who can accomplish miracles—but that takes money too!)

So please take our advice, start sending out those applications, and save. Invest wisely and consistently, and live with the knowledge that growing old can be financially rewarding and enjoyable.

IF HEINZ HAS 57 VARIETIES, BASKIN-ROBBINS SERVES 31 FLAVORS, AND MAX FACTOR HAS 97 SHADES OF LIPSTICK . . .

How Many Companies Offer DRIPs?

This appendix is designed for those of you who fall into one of the following categories: (a) You can't get those barbecue potato chip stains off your fingers in order to write for an application; (b) you are the king or queen of procrastinators; or (c) your easy chair is a little too comfortable, and you can't make it to the post office.

You see, not only have we given you the addresses of some of the companies that are offering DRIPs, we have even given you their telephone numbers.

Get into your favorite chair, pile up those snacks, and buy a speaker phone. Why? 'Cause you can request the application and prospectus over the phone!

P.S. Some of the companies have plan agents to administer their Dividend Re-Investment Plan, so direct your correspondence and request to the agent in order to save time.

Have fun and start phoning *now!*

AFLAC
holding company with
insurance and broadcasting
interests
1932 Wynnton Rd.
Columbus, GA 31999

Plan Agent:
Columbus Bank & Trust
(800) 227-4756

Initial—$750
Additional—$50

ALBERTSON'S INC
Grocery Chain
250 E. Parkcenter Blvd.
Boise, ID 83706

Plan Agent:
Chemical Trust
(800) 982-7649

Initial—15 shares
Additional—$10

AMERICAN WATER WORKS
water company
1025 Laurel Oak Rd.
Voorhees, NJ 08043

Plan Agent:
First National Bank Boston
(800) 736-3001

Initial—$100
Additional—$100

AMOCO
international oil company
200 E. Randolph Dr.
Chicago, IL 60601

Plan Agent:
First Chicago
(800) 446-2617

Initial—$450
Additional—$50

ATLANTIC ENERGY
utility holding company, owns
Atlantic City Energy
6801 Black Horse Pike
Pleasantville, NJ 08232
(609) 645-4506

Initial—$250
Additional—$10

ATMOS ENERGY
distributes natural gas
1800 Three Lincoln Ctr.
5430 LBJ Fwy.
Dallas, TX 75240

Plan Agent:
Bank of Boston
(800) 543-3038

Initial—$200
Additional—$25
IRA available

BANCORP HAWAII
regional bank holding
130 Merchant St.
Honolulu, HI 96813
(808) 537-8111
(808) 537-8239

Initial—1 share
Additional—$20

BARNETT BANKS
Florida's largest bank holding
company
50 N. Laura St.
Jacksonville, FL 32202-3638

Plan Agent:
First Chicago
(800) 808-2233

Initial—$250
Additional—$25
IRA available

BOB EVANS FARMS
sausage producer, restaurants
3776 S. High St.
Columbus, OH 43207-0863
(800) 272-7675

Initial—$50
Additional—$10

BOSTON EDISON
utility company
800 Bolyston St.
Boston, MA 02199-8003
(800) 736-3001

Plan Agent:
First National Bank of Boston
(800) 442-2001

Initial—$100
Additional—$10

BROOKLYN UNION GAS
distributor of natural gas
One MetroTech Ctr.
Brooklyn, NY 11201-3851
(718) 403-2000
(718) 403-3334

Initial—$250
Additional—$50

CAMPBELL SOUP
food
Campbell Pl.
Camden, NJ 08103
(609) 342-4800 ext. 2114

Plan Agent:
First Chicago
(201) 324-0498

Initial—1 share
Additional—$25

CAPSTEAD MORTGAGE
real estate investment trusts
2711 N. Haskell Ave.
Dallas, TX 75204
(214) 874-2323
(800) 526-7844

Initial—1 share
Additional—$50

CAROLINA POWER & LIGHT
southeastern utility company
411 Fayetteville St.
Raleigh, NC 27601
(919) 546-6111
(800) 662-7232

Initial—$20
Additional—$20

CENTERIOR ENERGY
utility company
P.O. Box 94661
Cleveland, OH 44101-4661
(216) 447-3100
(800) 433-7794

Initial—1 share
Additional—$10
IRA available

CENTRAL & SOUTH WEST
utility holding company
1616 Woodall Rodgers Fwy.
Dallas, TX 75202
(214) 777-1000
(800) 527-5797

Initial—$250
Additional—$25

CENTRAL HUDSON GAS &
ELECTRIC
utility company
284 South Ave.
Poughkeepsie, NY 12601-4879
(914) 452-2000

Initial—$100
Additional—$100

CENTRAL MAINE POWER
utility company
83 Edison Dr.
Augusta, ME 04336
(207) 623-3521
(800) 695-4267

Initial—1 share
Additional—$10

CENTRAL VERMONT PUBLIC
SERVICE
electric utility company
77 Grove St.
Rutland, VT 05701
(802) 773-2711
(802) 747-5406

Initial—$50
Additional—$50

CMS ENERGY
utility holding company
Fairlane Plaza S.
Suite 1100
3300 Town Center Dr.
Dearborn, MI 48126
(313) 436-9261
(517) 788-1868

Initial—$500
Additional—$25

COMSAT
telecommunications
6560 Rock Spring Dr.
Bethesda, MD 20817
(301) 214-3000
(301) 214-3200

Plan Agent:
Bank of New York
(800) 524-4458

Initial—$250
Additional—$50

CONNECTICUT ENERGY
gas utility company
855 Main St.
Bridgeport, CT 06604
(203) 579-1732
(800) 736-3001

Initial—$100
Additional—$50
IRA available

DAYTON HUDSON
clothing
777 Nicollet Mall
Minneapolis, MN 55402

Plan Agent:
First Chicago Trust
(800) 446-2617

Initial—1 share
Additional—$10

DEAN WITTER, DISCOVER
finance
Two World Trade Center
New York, NY 10048
(212) 392-2222
(800) 228-0829

Initial—$1,000
Additional—$100

DIAL CORPORATION
consumer household and food
products
Dial Tower
Phoenix, AZ 85077-1424
(800) 453-2235

Initial—$100
Additional—$10

DOMINION RESOURCES
electric utilities
901 E. Byrd St.
Richmond, VA 23261-6532
(804) 775-5700
(800) 552-4034

Initial—1 share
Additional—$10

DTE
electric utility
2000 Second Ave.
Detroit, MI 48226
(313) 237-8000
(800) 551-5009

Initial—$100
Additional—$25

DQE
electric utility
500 Cherrington Pkwy.
Coraopolis, PA 15108
(412) 262-4700
(800) 247-0400

Initial—$100
Additional—$10

DUKE POWER
electric utility
422 S. Church St.
Charlotte, NC 28242
(704) 594-0887
(800) 488-3853

Initial—$25
Additional—$25

EASTERN COMPANY
security products
112 Bridge St.
Naugatuck, CT 06770-2903
(203) 729-2255 x 241

Initial—$250
Additional—$50

ENERGEN CORPORATION
gas utility
2101 Sixth Ave. N.
Birmingham, AL 35203
(205) 326-2700
(800) 654-3206

Initial—$250
Additional—$25

EXXON CORPORATION
225 E. John W. Carpenter Fwy.
Irving, TX
75062-2298
(214) 444-1900

Plan Agent:
Bank of Boston
(800) 252-1800

Initial—$250
Additional—$50
IRA available

FLORIDA PROGRESS
electric utility
Barnett Tower
One Progress Plaza
St. Petersburg, FL 33701
(813) 824-6400
(813) 824-6416

Initial—$100
Additional—$10

FOOD LION, INC.
food related
2110 Executive Dr.
Salisbury, NC 28144
(704) 633-8250

Plan Agent:
Wachovia Bank
(800) 633-4236

Initial—1 share
Additional—$10

GENERAL MILLS
food
Number 1 General Mills Blvd.
Minneapolis, MN 55426
(612) 540-3888

Initial—1 share
Additional—$10

GILLETTE COMPANY
consumer products
Prudential Tower Building
Boston, MA 02199

Plan Agent:
First National Bank of Boston
(800) 730-4001

Initial—1 share
Additional—$10

GREEN MOUNTAIN POWER
electric utility
25 Green Mountain Dr.
South Burlington, VT 05402
(802) 864-5731

Initial—1 share
Additional—$50

HAWAIIAN ELECTRIC
utility company
900 Richards St.
Honolulu, HI 96813
(808) 532-5841

Initial—$100
Additional—$25

HEINZ
food
600 Grant St.
Pittsburgh, PA 15219
(412) 236-8000

Plan Agent:
Mellon Bank
(800) 253-3399

Initial—1 share
Additional—$25

HERSHEY FOODS
food
100 Crystal A Dr.
Hershey, PA 17033-0810
(717) 534-6799

Plan Agent:
Chemical Bank
(800) 851-4216

Initial—1 share
Additional—$50

HOME DEPOT
building materials
2727 Paces Ferry Rd.
Atlanta, GA 30339
(800) 928-0380

Initial—$250
Additional—$25

HOUSTON INDUSTRIES
electric utility
5 Post Oak Park

4400 Post Oak Pkwy.
Houston, TX 77027
(713) 629-3060

Initial—$250
Additional—$50

IDAHO POWER
electric utility
1221 W. Idaho St.
Boise, ID 83702-5627
(208) 388-2200
(800) 635-5406

Initial—1 share
Additional—$10

J.C. PENNEY
department store
P.O. Box 10001
Dallas, TX 75301
(214) 431-1000

Plan Agent:
Chemical Bank
(800) 345-3085

Initial—1 share
Additional—$20

KELLOGG COMPANY
food
P.O. Box 3599
Battle Creek, MI 49016-3599
(616) 961-2000

Plan Agent:
Harris Trust
(800) 323-6138

Initial—1 share
Additional—$25

KELLWOOD
textiles
600 Kellwood Pkwy.
St. Louis, MO 63178
(314) 576-3350

Initial—$100
Additional—$25

KERR-MCGEE
oil and gas
P.O. Box 25861
Oklahoma City, OK 73125
(405) 270-1313
(800) 395-2662

Initial—$750
Additional—$10

LIZ CLAIBORNE, INC.
clothing
1 Claiborne Ave.
North Bergen, NJ 07047
(201) 662-6000

Plan Agent:
First Chicago Trust
(201) 324-0498

Initial—1 share
Additional—$10

MADISON GAS & ELECTRIC
utility
133 S. Blair St.
Madison, WI 53701-1231
(800) 356-6423

Initial—$50
Additional—$25

McCORMICK & CO.
food
18 Loveton Circle
Sparks, MD 21152-6000
(410) 771-7301
(800) 424-5855

Initial—1 share
Additional—$100

MCDONALD'S
food
McDonald's Plaza
Oak Brook, IL 60521

Plan Agent:
First Chicago Trust
(800) 228-9623

Initial—$1,000
Additional—$100

MINNESOTA POWER &
LIGHT
electric utility
30 W. Superior St.
Duluth, MN 55802
(218) 722-2641
(218) 723-3974

Initial—1 share
Additional—$10

MOBIL CORPORATION
oil and gas
3225 Gallows Rd.
Fairfax, VA 22037-0001
(703) 846-3000

Plan Agent:
Chase Mellon
(800) 648-9291

Initial—$250
Additional—$10
IRA available

MONTANA POWER
electric and gas utility
40 E. Broadway
Butte, MT 59701-9989
(406) 723-5421
(800) 245-6767

Initial—$100
Additional—$10

MORTON INTERNATIONAL
chemicals
100 N. Riverside Plaza
Chicago, IL 60606-1596

Plan Agent:
First Chicago
(800) 990-1010

Initial—$200
Additional—$25
IRA available

NEVADA POWER
electric utility
6226 W. Sahara Ave.
Las Vegas, NV 89102
(702) 367-5000
(800) 344-9239

Initial—$25
Additional—$25

NEW YORK STATE
ELECTRIC & GAS
utility
P.O. Box 3287

Ithaca, NY 14851-3287
(607) 347-4131
(800) 225-5643

Initial—1 share
Additional—$25

OKLAHOMA GAS &
ELECTRIC COMPANY
utility
101 N. Robinson
Oklahoma City, OK 73101-0321
(405) 553-3000
(800) 395-2662

Initial—$250
Additional—$25
IRA available

PIEDMONT NATURAL GAS
gas company
P.O. Box 33068
Charlotte, NC 28233

Plan Agent:
Wachovia Bank
(800) 633-4236

Initial—$250
Additional—$25

PINNACLE WEST
utility
P.O. Box 52133
Phoenix, AZ 85072-2133
(800) 457-2983

Initial—$50
Additional—$10

PORTLAND GENERAL
electric utility
121 S.W. Salmon St.
Portland, OR 97204

Plan Agent:
First Chicago
(201) 324-0498

Initial—$250
Additional—$25
IRA available

PROCTER & GAMBLE
consumer goods
One Procter & Gamble Pl.
Cincinnati, OH 45202
(800) 742-6253

Initial—$100
Additional—$100

QUAKER OATS
food
Quaker Tower
321 N. Clark St.
Chicago, IL 60610
(312) 222-7111

Plan Agent:
Harris Trust
(800) 344-1198

Initial—1 share
Additional—$10

READERS DIGEST ASSOC.,
INC.
periodicals
Pleasantville, NY 10570
(914) 238-1000
(800) 242-4653

Initial—$1,000
Additional—$100

REGIONS FINANCIAL
banking
P.O. Box 1448
Montgomery, AL 36102-1448
(800) 638-6431

Initial—$20
Additional—$20

SARA LEE
food
Three First National Plaza
Chicago, IL 60602-4260
(312) 726-2600

Plan Agent:
Harris Savings
(312) 461-3932

Initial—1 share
Additional—$10

SCANA
electric & natural gas
1426 Main St.
Columbia, SC 29201
(803) 748-3000

Initial—$250
Additional—$25

SEARS, ROEBUCK AND CO.
retailer
Sears Tower
Chicago, IL 60684
(312) 875-2500

Plan Agent:
First Chicago
(800) 732-7780

Initial—1 share
Additional—$25

SMUCKER
food
Strawberry Lane
Orrville, OH 44667
(216) 682-3000

Plan Agent:
National City Bank
(800) 622-6757

Initial—1 share
Additional—$20

TENNECO
oil company
P.O. Box 2511
Houston, TX 77252-2511

Plan Agent:
First Chicago
(800) 446-2617

Initial—$500
Additional—$50

TEXACO
oil company
2000 Westchester Ave.
White Plains, NY 10650
(800) 283-9785

Initial—$250
Additional—$50

TYSON FOODS, INC.
food
2210 Oaklawn Dr.
Springdale, AR 72764

Plan Agent:
First Chicago
(800) 317-4445

Initial—$250
Additional—$50

U.S. WEST
telecommunications
7800 E. Orchard Rd.
Englewood, CO 80111

Initial—$300
Additional—$25

UTIL CORP UNITED
utility
P.O. Box 13287
Kansas City, MO 64199-3287

Plan Agent:
First Chicago
(800) 884-5426

Initial—$250
Additional—$50
IRA available

WAL-MART
department store
702 S.W. 8th St.
Bentonville, AR 72716
(501) 273-4000

Initial—$250
Additional—$50

WENDY'S
food
4288 W. Dublin-Granville Rd.
Dublin, OH 43017-0256

Plan Agent:
American Stock Transfer
(212) 936-5100

Initial—1 share
Additional—$20

WESTERN RESOURCES
electric & gas utility
818 Kansas Ave.
Topeka, KS 66601

Initial—$250
Additional—$20

WISCONSIN ENERGY
utility
231 W. Michigan St.
Milwaukee, WI 53201

Initial—$50
Additional—$25

WPS RESOURCES
utility
700 N. Adams St.
Green Bay, WI 54307-9001
(800) 236-1551

Initial—$100
Additional—$25

WRIGLEY
chewing gum
410 N. Michigan Ave.
Chicago, IL 60611
(312) 644-2121
(800) 824-9681

Initial—1 share
Additional—$50

APPENDIX B

SUGGESTED READING

The Beardstown Ladies. *The Beardstown Ladies Common Sense Investment Guide.* New York: Hyperion, 1994.

Berger, Esther, C.F.P. *Money Smart: Take the Fear out of Financial Planning.* New York: Avon Books, 1993.

Carlson, Charles B. C.F.A. *No-Load Stock.* New York: Mc-Graw Hill, 1995.

Carlson, Charles C.F.A. *Buying Stocks Without a Broker.* New York: McGraw-Hill, 1992.

Chilton, David. *The Wealthy Barber.* Rocklin, Calif.: Prima Publishing, 1996.

Drip Investor
(Newsletter)
published by NorthStar
Financial, Inc.
Calumet Avenue
Suite 200
Hammond, IN 46324-2692

Lowenstein, Roger. *Buffett—The Making of an American Capitalist.* New York: Random House, 1995.

Lynch, Peter and John Rothchild. *Learn to Earn.* New York: Fireside, 1995.

McGraw-Hill Companies. *Directory of Dividend Reinvestment Plans.* 1995 Edition.

Sease, Douglas, and John Presbo. *Barron's Guide to Making Investment Decisions.* New York: Prentice Hall, 1994.

The Wall Street Journal. Guide to Understanding Money & Investing. New York: Lightbulb Press, Inc., 1992.

Warfield, Gerald. *How to Read and Understand the Financial News.* New York: Harper Perennial, 1994.

Notes

Notes

Notes

Notes